ISBN: 9781973121923

-ooOOoo-

TABLE OF CONTENTS

RHYMING WORDS ARE FOR EVERYONE?

They make us feel happy, or sad; at times they bring comfort and sometimes pain, but always they are a joy to the soul. The best rhyming words are not the complicated ones full of big words that writhe and snake about as you try to come to terms with their meaning.

The very best rhyming words are simple and clean, pure, and sometimes they can cut like a knife. They can make you laugh, they can make you angry, they can say what you feel and often they can tell the world what you are trying to hide – more clearly than you might imagine. Sometimes they can make you cry. There are rhyming words in this book that can do all of these things, in different ways, to different people at different times. It is important that everyone is touched by rhyming words at some point in their life, for a life without them is no life at all. Sometimes they don't even have to rhyme. Sometimes they just have to be words that say the right thing, to the right person.

This is not poetry. We never use the P word, because everyone immediately assumes you're trying to be clever. The P word is not allowed in this book – we only ever whisper it anyway because it assumes a life of its own if you speak it loudly. It changes its shape and form and meaning, step by arrogant step, until it no longer spells poetry. It spells pretentious instead. I'm not sure what that means, but it doesn't sound good to me, so here there are only…

Rhyming words (or words that don't even rhyme).

It's all about what the words mean to you. Nobody else can ever see the things you see in exactly the way you see them. It can be the most enlightening and surprising thing to just sit quietly, away from all the noise and interruptions, and just read some rhyming words. Try it. It's true. No one else needs to know, and I won't tell them. Promise.

ALONE

The milkman calls at six fifteen, the postman calls at ten,
But no one pays a visit 'til the milkman calls again;
The aged eyes are rheumy and the thinning hair is white,
Yet not a soul will knock the door to see if he's alright;
Each day is spent reflecting on the things he's seen and done,
And wond'ring if he'll still be here to see tomorrow's sun.
There's no one there to speak to, to comfort or berate,
So he watches all the schoolkids as they pass down by the gate;
The district nurse goes by at noon, driving up the lane,
And twenty minutes later, she drives on past again.
The rheumy eyes sit watching but there's not a soul to see,
Until the cat from down the road arrives at ten past three;
The milk is quickly taken and the cat is on his way,
Leaving yet more loneliness with which to fill the day.
The afternoon is waning as the evening filters in,
Adding livid shadows to the face's wrinkled skin;
The rheumy eyes are sunken into pools of deep despair,
As he goes into the garden, to take the evening air.
The summer night is chilly so it's off to bed he goes,
And as he pulls his nightshirt on he dwells on what he knows –
The milkman calls at six fifteen the postman calls at ten,
But no one pays a visit 'til the milkman calls again…

-ooOOoo-

THE SONG OF THE SWORD

In the pain of the furnace my body was forged,
     Longer than life have I been;
The fury of battle is where I have gorged,
     On kidney and liver and spleen;
You think me a trinket so prettily shown,
     Yet many's the life I have claimed;
Parting the sinew and hewing the bone,
     My mercy is leaving you maimed;
In hope I was wrought and in anger unsheathed,
     Blood flows like wine where I've played;
I'm promised to Death and to Chaos bequeathed,
     For I am the Devil's own blade.

Oh thou fool if only you could see the sights I've seen,
If only you'd experienced the places I have been;
I rode the Steppes of Russia on the horse of Genghis Khan,
And hacked and slew the peasants on the roads to Kazakhstan.
I've taken life of woman and I've taken life of child,
And watched them rape survivors ere their temples were defiled;
Then in the hands of Subotai I sang the reaper's song,
To cross the frozen Volga drinking blood all winter long.

I swam the Sajo river to a feast of rended flesh,
And slashed the fleeing Magyars as they ran into our mesh;
I faced the hordes of China as the Kerulen they crossed,
To share the bitter anguish of my Mongols who were lost.
I passed in trade for silver to a Christian warrior's child,
Who carried me across the sea of waves so fierce and wild;
The long years of his childhood I was idle save for show,
But lo – he grew to manhood so it's off to war we go!

We crossed the heaving waters in a hundred years of war,
To visit our destruction on a place called Agincourt;
And when the French attacked our camp in vain malicious hope,
I slew three score of prisoners securely bound in rope.
I've hacked and stabbed the Scottish and the Welsh on mountains blue,
And paid in chinking golden coins I've killed some English too;
I've disembowelled the Irish at Drogheda and The Boyne,
And seen them staked and screaming as the knife cuts out the groin.

Across the Himalayas I've killed tribesmen by the score,
And marched them all upon my point to yield their winter store;
In lofty mountain passes countless thousands have I slain,
But still the fools come on that I may taste them yet again.
I've backed them into holes and caves and slaughtered every one,
And where I cleave no man may breathe that I have touched upon;
They've carried me in hatred and in dying laid me down,
Then placed me gleaming on his chest whilst bearing him through town.

I've razed the shining city and I've laid the temple low,
For none may see what I have seen or know what I may know;
My cutting edge has bitten deep in smashed and bloodied breasts,
And burst upon the banquet as the host has slain his guests.
I've cut the Sikh to ribbons in the pass at Kandahar,
And watched the rebels boiled in oil and dipped in molten tar;
I've fought and slain the Moguls and the Afghan in his turn,
And slew the Turk so often I believe he'll never learn.

I've sacked and pillaged cities where the children called us names,
How often have I left their bodies burning in the flames;
I've been the pain of mothers and the hate of grieving wives,
And witnessed strong men beg for death beneath the red-hot knives.
I served the Lord Protector in his strong and steady hand,
How proudly did he raise me as his tool to tame the land;
Often I have revelled in the blood of countless foes,
Just to spite the mother's pride I've hewed the daughter's nose.

I've been the bane of bandits and at times the bane of law,
At times I've taken rich men and at times I took the poor;
I've spilled warm blood in virgin snow and drained it into sand,
I smashed Marsin at Blenheim and Sanjar at Samarkand.
Behind me there is weal and woe in front just naked dread,
On either side for mile on mile are piles of butchered dead;
To beat me into farmyard tools is often heard the threat,
But I've been here forever and I'm not a ploughshare yet!

Wherever there was ringing steel it's there I've tasted blood,
For on the raging ramparts of Granada have I stood;
I've watched the blazing campfires of my enemies at night,
But come the morn when I am drawn I'm sharp and gleaming bright.
They've polished me with sharkskin and they've burnished me with care,
And cleaned the blood from cutting edge with locks of corpses hair;
I held the bridge at Pedu and the gates at Chandrapur,
And finished off the wounded in the streets of Bangalore.

I've hacked my way through living flesh and gloried in the stench,
Or watched on from my scabbard as my master raped a wench;
I charged the guns at Waterloo and smashed in many a head,
Upon the morning after I watched peasants loot the dead.
My path is strewn with corpses for my tally's long and deep,
I've known the weak man lose his mind and seen the strong man weep;
I've watched the blue ranks break and run and rushed to hunt them down,
And seen their lifeblood cloak them in a sodden scarlet gown.

I've heard the keening grapeshot as it thunders through the air,
And when they charged the Russian guns my gleaming blade was there.
I've taken life in anger and I've taken life in fun,
And watched the bloodied grass glow red in many a morning sun;
From Omdurman to Crecy – from Kabul to Chandrapur,
I've seen them run like women or come on to take some more.
But always there is carnage on the sullied fields of death,
And often there is knowledge as they draw that final breath.

You dare to wear me casually for you are but a boy,
And show me off when on parade as though I were a toy.
You thrill the pretty ladies with the stories from your lips,
And little do you contemplate the killer at your hips.
Resplendent in your uniform you swagger to the mess,
To talk of fights and battles at which you can only guess.
You think to boast of slaying with your tales of blood and gore?
How little do you know, oh fool, speak not to **_me_** of war!

-ooOOOoo-

ACT OF FOOLISHNESS

The day is slow and sullen with a sky of leaden sheet,
A drizzled mist swirls grimly round the people in the street;
How little you have altered since the time I saw you last,
And though I wish the scene would change it seems the die is cast.

So casually we sit and chat avoiding awkward themes,
And if the conversation wanes the mood is strained it seems;
Infrequently you visit now for we are only 'friends',
Neither sure where 'friendship' starts or where the loving ends.

Like strangers acting out a play we both must tread the boards,
Yet now the house is empty and no audience applauds;
There's just the hollow echo of our bickering and lies,
Playing parts for no one to avoid each other's eyes.

Our halting lines are jumbled yet my thoughts are right on cue,
If I live to be a thousand I could not get over you;
But both of us are giving the performance of our life,
Screaming in our silence at the twisting of the knife.

We wound each other grievously before the curtain falls,
Bowing like the fools we are towards the empty stalls;
A wave to each deserted box then blow each one a kiss,
Please tell me so I understand – how did we come to this?

THE SEASONS OF MAN

Spring:

Each passing day brings its sorrows and cares,
Weekends bring pleasure and joy;
For schooling is dull when the fields are aflame,
And the man is yet but a boy.

The weights are not yet on his shoulders,
Life's cares have not furrowed the brow;
The furnace of youth burns so bright and so hot
When the arms have not tended the plough.

Eyes that are warm and alert and alive,
A mind that is eager to learn;
A confidence born of naïve self-belief,
And a trust that is easy to earn.

Each living hour is a magic adventure,
Brimming with colour and life;
Limbs that are growing in strength and in vigour,
Senses as sharp as a knife.

Values untainted by greed and by malice,
A face that can never deceive;
Cheerfully safe and secure in the knowledge
It's better to give than receive.

Yet the man from the boy is emerging,
The chrysalis cracks with the strain;
Ambition is whispering deep in the psyche,
Stronger with each growing pain.

Opinions that form like the forests and seas,
Sturdy and upright and strong,
Ideals that spring forth in a burst of conviction,
Distortions of right and of wrong.

The shutters have fallen and light floods within,
Naiveté loses the war;
Thunder and lightning is rending the soul and behold –
The boy is no more.

Summer:

The strength of a man is a brew to be savoured,
Coursing the body like wine;
The mind is a tool to be used for advantage,
Selecting the grapes from the vine.

The seed that was planted now stands strong and tall,
The eyes are now judging and deep;
The lion springs forth from the kitten of boyhood,
Ready to sow and to reap.

The thoughts and the fears and the hopes and illusions,
Swaying like wind-ruffled corn;
Each tossing ear bearing grain for the future,
In summer no hope is forlorn.

The girl watches on from the stooks in the fields,
His scythe dances on through the wheat;
Shoulders are swaying and sinews are taut,
Gold in the shimmering heat.

A long summer's eve by the banks of the pool,
The lion enjoying his soak;
The girl saunters past with a smile on her lips
And the lion is tamed at a stroke.

Now is the time of enchantment and dreams,
A time when time seems to fly;
Two lovers are dancing entwined in the moonlight,
Under the velvety sky.

Two chemistries merge and the magic floods forth,
This time comes but once in a life;
Love burns white hot on both sides of the coin
And the young man will take him a wife.

The world he will change and the seas he will drain,
Passion comes in at the trot;
The older men sigh and stare blankly at space,
For they know what young men do not.

The path is a long one and littered with flints,
But nevertheless it's begun;
Three harvests have passed in the field by the pool,
Now proudly he cradles his son.

The thoughts and the dreams pass like clouds in the sky,
Slipping like sand through the glass;
And though he will hunt them and try to entrap them,
Somehow they manage to pass.

Another four harvests have stood in the field,
A daughter now lies in the cot;
And though he's as pleased and as proud as can be,
The sun is now not quite so hot.

Autumn:

Ambitions and fancies that burned like the sun
Are kept at a comfortable heat;
And though there are times when he dreams of the lion
His mind is kept busy with wheat.

With three other mouths he must feed and protect,
His time is no longer his own;
The wine in his veins is no longer as potent,
He shoulders the scythe with a groan.

The stout winter store is well stocked to the rafters,
His labours went well it would seem;
And down in the meadow his son and his daughter
Are tickling trout in the stream.

The colours are changing all over the land,
A golden and russet array;
His step's not as quick and the hair of his head
Is tinged with a silvery grey.

At times he is quiet and wistful and distant,
Thoughtful of what might have been;
Smoking his pipe in the chair by the fireside,
Or giving his scythe blade a clean.

The grass on the pasture needs baling for hay,
His son holds the twine for each knot;
And though all the great dreams lie shattered and broken
He dwells on the riches he's got.

The girl with the brown hair and strawberry lips,
Is grooming a horse in the barn;
The boy with the devilment deep in his eyes;
Is helping to knot baling yarn.

But dearest of all is the girl from the poolside,
Many a harvest ago;
When she gives him that look and her lips start to curl,
He feels that warm inner glow.

The cool autumn airs shroud the banks of the stream,
Two lovers walk down by the pool;
Spellbound he watches them glide through the mists,
Reflecting how life can be cruel.

The lovers embrace as they tenderly kiss,
In almost the very same spot;
The man heaves a sigh as he looks to the heavens,
For he knows what young men do not.

The autumn of man is a time of much splendour,
Of counting the fruits of the field;
Of storing the same with one eye for the future,
Ambition is starting to yield.

The path that he treads that was once strewn with flints,
Is worn to the polish of tile;
Each load he has shouldered and borne by his strength,
Has flattened it mile upon mile.

Each turn from the path that he once yearned to walk,
Seems hostile and unsafe to tread;
What once seemed a challenge is fraught with unease,
Where once there was fire there is dread.

Yet still he will glory in what he's achieved,
Complacent in what he's become;
He may not be rich, but life has its comforts,
Plain, but better than some.

Look out to the hills and the far off horizons,
Bringing their portents of ill;
For autumn is leaving in golden procession,
Breezes are grating and chill.

Winter:
Beneath leaden skies come the flurries of rain,
Speaking of snows yet to fall;
While down in the barn unaware of the maelstrom,
The girl tends her horse in its stall.

The boy heaves a spade in the vigour of youth,
Clearing the ditches for flood;
The man sweats and blows as he swings with an axe,
Chopping and stacking the wood.

His wife fills her jars with the pickles and jams,
Smiling with pride and delight;
The purple-black sky comes alive with fresh snowflakes,
Bringing their mantle of white.

Long are the nights of the wintertide season,
Deep are the thoughts of a man;
Slow are his steps for his legs are unsteady,
Walking where once he had ran.

White is his hair and his face has grown wrinkled,
Rounded and knowing and kind;
But yet when his wife smiles across at her husband,
The lion stands proud in her mind.

The snows lie so thick on the roof of the house,
Jack Frost stalks the land like a thief;
But though he is feeble and weak in the body,
The man finds his strength in belief.

The long years have taken the grapes from his vineyard,
Sapping the strength of his wine;
And though he no longer can scythe in the wheatfield,
The old eyes with memories shine.

Gone are the dreams and the prevarications,
Gone is the gnawing self doubt;
Here is a mind that was tempered by decades,
Knowing what life is about.

Outside the icicles cling to the gutters,
Inside the fire warms the room;
The old eyes rest proudly on son and on daughter,
Struggling to pierce the gloom.

So what of the boy when the fields were aflame?
What of the man in his prime?
The lesson of life is not taught in a moment,
But only the fulness of time.

-ooOOoo-

FOR EVER

Two glances fused together as you glide on down the aisle,
I wonder if you'll think of me just once in every while?
Across the years I've watched and loved you, keeping it inside,
And now they've placed you out of reach as someone else's bride.
But it was always you.

No matter where life's compass steers or where its pathways lead,
I'll always be this empty for my soul will always bleed.
You've fllled my every waking hour – why is it you can't see?
Now I know my life's desire can never, ever be.
It is always you.

The hours we spent together are the mem'ries which will shine,
But all you will remember is you were a friend of mine;
Perhaps you'll wonder why I never visit any more,
Just one more friend who's cast adrift on time's forgotten shore.
It will always be you.

The times I've stood and talked with you and passed the time of
day,
The times I've hoped and prayed my eyes aren't giving me away;
The thoughts I've thought and dreams I've dreamed are choking in
my breast;
The whirling cauldron in this heart at which you've never guessed.
I will always love you.

The waiting now is over for the cards have all been turned,
The dice are thrown, the lifelines cut, and all the bridges burned;
There is no pain or anger – just a numbness deep inside,
Knowing as I look at you that part of me has died.
For ever.

-oo0O0oo-

FOR YOU

There's many things I dream of,
Whilst looking in your eyes,
Of happiness in days to come,
Of kisses and of sighs;
Your company I value,
Your loving oh so sweet,
Each time I see your smiling face,
This old heart skips a beat.
For all my life I've waited,
Watching just for you,
Your understanding sweetness,
Those eyes of sapphire blue;
Those little looks you give me,
Those sexy knowing smiles,
For each of your sweet kisses,
I'd walk a million miles.
I know that you were sent to me,
From heaven up above,
Just so I can hold you tight,
And give you all my love;
My sweetheart I must have you,
No matter what the cost,
For in my heart of hearts I know,
Without you I'd be lost.
I love you most because you're cute,
You know that this is true,
And if you ever went away,
You know that I'd be blue;
My moods may change and vary,
For better or for ill,
But when I'm old and ninety three,
You know I'll love you still.

-oooOooo-

THE PRICE OF A LOAF

"Pray fetch me a rope for this villain must hang,"
The Lord High Sheriff said;
"His crime has been proved and in blood he shall pay,
For stealing a loaf of bread."
The boy was composed for he spoke not a word,
Though his lips a'quivered in dread;
Then a voice from the crowd that could scarce be heard,
Said "let's 'ang the sheriff instead!"

The constables dived for the mutinous rogue,
But never a sniff did they get:
And sniggers were rife as the constables searched,
Red-faced and dripping with sweat.
Now after a time there was peace in the court,
The sheriff demanded a rope;
But yet again from the crowd came the voice,
"Sheriff you've no bloody 'ope!"

The uproar was vast and the constables grabbed,
Laughter welled up like a tide;
The sheriff went red and then purple with rage,
Speechless with mortified pride.
"Bring me the culprit" the bailiff cried out,
"So 'elp me I'll watch 'im swing;"
"Bugger you mate" said the voice in the crowd,
"You've more chance of 'angin' The King!"

The constables chivvied and poked with their staves,
The crowd was becoming a mob;
Above all the laughter the sheriff roared out,
"Bailiff get on with your job!"
"We can't 'old 'em back sir" the bailiff replied,
"P'raps we should call out the guard?"
And that they'd have done if they possibly could,
But the way from the courtroom was barred.

"Surrender or die" said the voice in the crowd,
Vainly the men formed in rank;
Meanwhile the sheriff had suffered a fit,
Features as stiff as a plank.
The scene had turned ugly and many a head
Was cracked by a constable's stave;
But in the confusion the boy in the dock,
Escaped from his premature grave.

A week to the day saw the sheriff's farewell,
The seizure had cost him his life;
No one could say who had spoke from the crowd,
Though rumour and gossip was rife.
The youth had slipped quietly off with the fair,
Back to the job of his choice;
Earning his bread in the sideshows and stalls,
Drinking whilst throwing his voice!

-ooOOoo-

THE FAR PLACE

I'm going to a far place where soft airs will kiss my face,
Where golden sun will wash away the pain;
To greet remembered faces with a tender warm embrace,
Where loving arms enfold me once again.

I'm going to a far place to wander through the trees,
Where soothing hands will wipe away my tears;
To taste the pine's sweet perfume as it lingers on the breeze,
Where whispered words caress the deepest fears.

I'm going to a far place full of washed-out skies of blue,
Where dreamily I'll walk each golden strand;
To rest awhile between the dunes or watch the sparkling dew,
Where knowing guides will lead me through the land.

I'm going to a far place where sweet laughter fills the air,
Where cheerful dancing feet tread lightly on;
To revel in the brightness and to run without a care,
Where doubt and dread and darkness are all gone.

I'm going to a far place with no shout or shrill demand,
Where only gentle words are softly said;
To wait for just one heartbeat until I can take your hand,
Where you will see I wasn't ever dead.

-oo0Ooo-

THE MAN WHO DRINKS ALONE

He's found in every public bar from Looe to Inverness,
The only solace he can find is in a glass I guess;
As moodily he gazes so intently at his beer,
Contemplating how much time it takes for it to clear;
The only time the pain is eased and sorrow overthrown,
Is when his mind is fogged with ale – the man who drinks alone.

The landlord glances over with his quick and knowing eyes,
While lending half an ear to the local drunkard's lies;
He wonders just what crushing weight can lay a man so low,
Then offers thanks to heaven for the fact he doesn't know;
Few may see the orchard where Despair's rank fruits are grown,
Yet one has tasted all of them – the man who drinks alone.

With bitterness and anguish and betrayal in his face,
With eyes devoid of feeling as they stare out into space;
He struggles through life's ether with the cross he has to bear,
Unknowing in his isolation, vacant in his stare;
He stumbles on in blindness, for so long it's all he's known,
Yet he's seen all he wants to see – the man who drinks alone.

Around him life goes marching on in timeless disarray,
As day turns into night-time and the night-time into day;
Each one a little longer than the one that came before,
No longer does he wonder what it is he's living for;
A long time back he sinned a sin and now he must atone,
Each night he pays the dreadful price – the man who drinks alone.

-ooOOoo-

THE PAEAN OF THE SMITTEN

What shall I write of thee my love,
Who matches me as hand to glove?
You read my moods and soothe my ire,
And pour thy love upon the fire
As gentle raindrops from above.

My soul is in thy keeping true,
For who knows me as well as you?
Who else has such bewitching eyes
To penetrate my poor disguise,
And steal my heart the way you do?

I love the things you do and say,
How did you learn to kiss that way?
Your laughter sweet as mountain air,
So fresh and clean and free from care
To make me love you more each day.

With adoration I am bound,
What is this paradise I've found?
Who is this vixen sometimes wild,
Who often treats me as a child
Yet has the power to astound?

You fill my every waking thought,
What is this lesson I've been taught?
My soul would starve were you not mine,
As grapes that wither on the vine,
For all my life it's you I've sought.

You hold me 'neath some wondrous spell,
And where it springs from who can tell?
How is it that you have this power
To grant me heaven in an hour,
Then roast my heart in flames of hell?

To thee I'm drawn as moth to flame,
How could I wish to end this game?
A willing slave to thy caprice
Yet never wishing for release,
Love's pain and pleasure each the same.

With thee close by the earth is still,
How could these eyes drink in their fill?
And should I ever seek to sate
This hunger which will not abate,
And ever bends me to thy will?

Thy beauty humbles each new morn,
Were you the reason I was born?
You show me caverns of delight,
And like the stars you fire the night,
Eclipsing moonbeams 'til the dawn.

We have no secrets you and I,
Why have you never told me why?
Could it be that we shall stand
Before God's altar hand in hand,
To have and hold what gold can't buy?

-oo0Ooo-

THE BALLAD OF TOMMY SHEARS

The red coats add their colour to the pretty village square,
And all the burghers of the land have rushed to gather there;
Great news we have to give, and greetings from the King,
The fife and drum do loudly play, and all the people sing.

Come take King George's shilling lads, for he has need of you,
The French are at it once again – come fight the coats of blue;
For British hearts are made from steel, and never known to yield,
Famed for valour, known for strength on every battlefield.

The barracks now are crowded with the young and strong and fit,
"We'll teach them froggies manners boys" says some incumbent wit;
But proudest of the whole brigade is little Tommy Shears,
A drummer in the fourteenth foot despite his tender years.

Young Tommy's only ten years old, his heart is full of fight,
His boots are black, his tunic red, his belt is pipeclay white;
He took the army's ninepence (for that's all he was allowed),
And soon he's off to fight in Spain to make his mother proud.

Yet in the pretty village Tommy's mother sits and weeps,
Her only child's a soldier boy whose lock of hair she keeps;
But Tommy knows no sorrow as he steps down off the dock,
His drum cries out its call to arms as steady as a rock.

The roads to Spain are dusty and the heat is even worse,
The weary and the footsore moan, around him grown men curse;
The little town is sleepy, far from Lisbon with its port,
The cobbled streets resounding as they march into the fort.

Then onwards through the hillsides, with woodsmoke in the air,
Young Tommy's drum still beating out to tell the French beware;
The mules haul up the cannons as they raise their choking dust,
The young boys take up cannon balls to chip away the rust.

Yet finally the column rests, the hooves have ceased to pound,
And Tommy helps the sergeant driving pegs into the ground;
The men are drawing water from a gushing little spring,
Each icy draught is nectar as it makes the dry throat sting.

The eve of battle beckons as the tents are rigged up tight,
The smells of cooking fill the air, dusk turns into night;
Pickets have been posted and the ale has been passed round,
And men sink slowly into sleep until there's not a sound.

The smells are strange and foreign to a country boy from Kent,
The clammy air is stifling in the closeness of the tent;
The sergeant sits alone bathed in the fire's ghostly light,
Fingering his musket as he contemplates the fight.

His soldier's senses stir him – for a second he's alarmed,
But why, 'tis only little Tom – alone and quite unarmed;
"Here have a piece o' sausage Tom, an' 'ave a mug o' beer,
You stick by me tomorrow son, we'll win through – never fear!"

The morning sun is fiery as it ravages the dark,
Revealing lines of scarlet coats, risen with the lark;
Come lift your musket, heft your pack, a marching line of red;
And with the colours, beating loud, is Tommy at their head.

Across the vale are lines of blue with cannons on the slope,
And cavalry with shining swords, Napoleon's greatest hope;
The cannons belch their thunder at the slender scarlet line,
And then the columns three by three come marching oh so fine.

The crackling of the muskets and the hideous screams of men,
The thund'ring of the horse's hooves – and back they come again;
The heat and sweat and fear and rage are mingled with the blood,
And many a horse and many a man plunge headlong in the mud.

Through all the battle's fury, with eyes a blazing bright,
Young Tommy beats his precious drum, and keeps the timing right;
His face is creased and blackened and the colour's like a rag,
Yet still he stands to beat the time beneath the union flag.

His little hands are aching and his feet are wracked with pain,
Each roll another mile to run, etched into his brain;
For near two hours his sticks have danced without the merest pause,
And up the hill he's led them – to the cannon's gaping jaws.

The keening shriek of metal makes the air vibrate and howl,
Blending with the clash of blades, the musket's snapping growl;
The fighting now is hand to hand, the blood it flows like wine,
The grass becomes a scarlet rug beneath the thin red line.

The cannons have been carried and the French are in retreat,
But where, amongst the battle's noise, is Tommy's steady beat?
As twilight hides the carnage and the wounded cry and moan,
A sergeant carefully searches with a sinking heart of stone.

Beneath a cannon's limber lies the battle's choicest toll,
The lifeless form of Tommy Shears, a shattered scarlet doll;
Tenderly the big man stoops to check the little boy,
His great big heart is breaking as he lifts him like a toy.

The morrow was a Sunday with a sunrise bright and clear,
And though it was a victory proud, the price had cost them dear;
Upon the peaceful hillside they laid Tommy deep in bed,
Wrapped in the tattered union flag that had fluttered o'er his head.

-ooOOOoo-

THE MORTUARY KEEPER

The face is lined and weary from fatigue and lack of sleep,
  Her tears have dried to tracks of finest lace;
The widow walks the mortuary her job it is to keep,
  Compassion etched upon her simple face.
Her measured tread is heavy with the crushing weight she bears,
  Yet of the pain within there's not a sign;
Though war has scourged and flayed her there's no effort that she spares,
  To soothe each broken body in the line.
The ship had been torpedoed but had limped back into port,
  The precious cargo stood upon the dock;
But all the sailors trapped below had died where they were caught,
  Faces set in masks of fear and shock.
The widow's patient hands reach out to straighten ruffled hair,
  Her husband was torpedoed just last year;
And as she bends to smooth a brow her eyes are filled with care,
  Betraying with a solitary tear.
The fourteenth table is the last and now her legs grow weak,
  A fair-haired youth of barely seventeen;
So tenderly the widow stoops to kiss the icy cheek,
  To touch the boyish face so smooth and clean.
Who would blame the widow for the aching in her breast?
  Who can know the web of grief that's spun?
And who can say she tended him more gently than the rest?
  Even though the young boy was her son.

-oooOOooo-

THE WINDOW IN THE CAVE

When I came home this evening there was sullen passive ire,
The heating hadn't worked all through the day;
Unless I fixed it quick the repercussions would be dire,
Her foot was tapping in that *special* way.

Having found the problem there was warmth in the abode,
It only took an hour or two to fix;
Still she wasn't happy, though the message was in code,
Tons of metaphoric falling bricks.

Perhaps I'm unreceptive or not listening as I should,
Suggested by the daggers in her look;
Finally the shaft of light comes ambling through the wood,
In the cave, it's far too dark to cook.

She needs a nice new window so the light can enter in,
Pointing at the pre-selected site;
Make sure as you cut, you put the rubbish in the bin,
Have it done by eight o'clock tonight.

Try to keep the noise down 'cos she wants to have a rest,
Off I trot to fetch the tools I need;
To cut a nice new window in the wall that faces west,
In the very spot we have agreed.

A long and sweaty labour are the hammer's driving blows,
Dust swirls in the air to send me blind;
Stopping every minute so that I can blow my nose,
Before returning to the weary grind.

Finally it's done and blessed light floods in the cave,
Masonry and dust is cleared away;
Looking through the window I see trees and grasses wave,
Here within is bright and clear as day.

She comes in to inspect the work with light and airy skip,
But all is not quite as it ought to be;
The view could be much better - gritted teeth and sneering lip,
The bushes make it difficult to see.

Maybe if the grass was mown or cut the bushes down,
Or maybe if the sun was not so bright;
She says it's sited wrongly with her condescending frown;
Fill it in – but finish it tonight!

She won't rest easy in her bed is what I hear her say,
To block it up with rock should be my goal;
And make the new one over there to look the other way,
It shouldn't take me long to make the hole;

The tools I need are waiting like true and faithful friends,
The rocks I need are nestling on the slope;
This is where the digging starts and where the cutting ends,
Where supplicating arms reach up for hope.

The dancing shafts of sunlight wander idly through the cave,
The window is a cheery golden sight;
Warming rays give witness to the mutiny of the slave,
The window's where I left it overnight.

I think the view is wonderful across the rolling ground,
And gleefully I savour my release;
Upon the grassy slope is seen a freshly piled mound,
And in the shed the shovel keeps its peace.

-ooO0Ooo-

THEY

They packed the leather briefcase with the papers they would need
  They took the man and placed him on a train;
On either side of him they sat with faces stern and grim,
  The three connected by a shiny chain.

The journey was a long one and the two spoke not a word,
  They knew each jolt of rail and sway of bend;
And though the men were silent as they sped along the track,
  Each knew well the fate at journey's end.

The plain black van was waiting as the train came to a halt,
  The uniforms were dark viewed through the gloom;
They walked him off across the platform, anxious to be gone,
  To flee the crowd who wondered at his doom.

They drove him to the prison where they locked him in a cell,
  They gave him soup then took his clothes away;
They gave him prison uniform and shoes without the ties,
  They told him they must watch him night and day.

The days were filled with boredom and the nights were long and
cold,
  They told him he had just a couple more;
They said he'd sinned a mighty sin by doing what he'd done,
  Now he must pay the penalty of law.

They measured him and weighed him but all he did was stare,
  They took his ring (but gave him a receipt);
And while they stretched a length of rope there came to him a priest,
  Forgiving him his anger and deceit.

They tried to reassure him in his purgatory of mind,
  Misunderstanding apathy for fear;
The night was long and silent as he made his private peace,
  Watching as the time drew ever near.

They came for him at daybreak with the frosty rays of dawn,
The faces pale, the hearts of solid ice;
They took him to the scaffold's maw and placed him in the noose,
And for his passion, there he paid the price.

-ooOOOoo-

Inspired by a photograph of Timothy Evans being taken to London by train, flanked by two detectives.

FROM A FATHER

Please teach me the ballad of Kirwan,
Oh father please tell me the tale,
Of how he was wrecked in the vast southern sea,
And driven for days by the gale.

"*My son it is long past your bedtime*",
Said father with hints of a smile;
"*But if you are quick on your way to your bunk,
I'll keep you amused for a while*".

The candle was guttering wildly,
As though in a storm out at sea;
Father sat down on the small wooden trunk,
And laughed for a moment at me.

His voice was so rich and so steady,
I still can recall it today:
I lay in my bunk snuggled in to the warm,
And listened for what he would say.

"*Now Kirwan was my father's uncle,
A mariner grizzled and tough;
His leathery face was all wrinkled and grained,
His hands were all calloused and rough.*

"*His sea-going skill was a legend,
He handled a ship like a toy;
His life had been spent on the oceans and seas,
Ever since he was a boy.*

"*He signed as the mate of the 'Plover',
A ship bound for Botany Bay;
I don't know the cargo and though I did ask,
My own father never would say.*

"The 'Plover' weighed anchor at Bristol,
And Kirwan was mostly in charge;
He knew that the ship had seen much better days,
And the crew wasn't fit for a barge.

"The ship clawed her way down the channel,
Away to the wide rolling seas;
The land fell behind as full canvas went up,
Trapping the soul of the breeze.

"Onward she sailed into Biscay,
With squalls so contrary and mean;
Wind sliced at rigging and waves marched in lines,
Mountains of shimmering green.

"The captain stayed lockcd in his cabin,
Sodden with brandy and ale;
Kirwan stayed up on the deck without sleep,
Watching the trim of each sail.

"A week and the bay was behind them,
And there was the Ivory Coast;
The African sun is a savage to bear,
Yet still Kirwan kept to his post.

"No one knew ought of the Captain,
Save for his staggering shape;
So Kirwan kept watch at the quarterdeck rail,
While 'Plover' was rounding the cape.

"By this stage our Kirwan was weary,
Knowing he must have some sleep;
So he staggered below while the bosun took watch,
For the shepherd must needs leave the sheep."

At this point I felt just like Kirwan,
Eyelids as heavy as lead;
Father was grinning and stroking his nose,
Making to go to his bed.

Oh father I'm not really sleepy,
In fact I'm not tired at all;
If you break off now I shall never be sure,
Whether this tale is tall!

Father leaned back with a chuckle,
Brushing his beard with a thumb;
*"If you think this tale is a tall one I've told,
Just listen to what is to come!*

*"Kirwan had fought like a tiger,
He slept for a day and two nights,
But when he awoke there was much work to do,
Putting the ship back to rights.*

*"Eleven full days Kirwan drove them,
Tarring and splicing the ropes;
Sailors sang songs under strange southern stars,
Happy and full of high hopes.*

*"Twas then that the giant squid found them,
Crushing and rending the ship;
The tentacles flailed each as thick as the mast,
Splintering planks in their grip.*

*"Masts shivered loud under protest,
Spars toppled down to the deck;
Lines snapped like twine as the tentacles squeezed,
'Plover' was now just a wreck.*

*"Gently she started to settle,
Water poured into the hold;
Masts snapped like twigs as the maindeck collapsed,
Slowly the old 'Plover' rolled.*

*"Air bubbles came to the surface,
The galley stove shot out its sparks;
Men cried aloud to their God as they thrashed,
Falling as prey to the sharks.*

"The few that survived huddled quietly,
Using smashed timbers to float;
Kirwan, as usual cool to the last,
Was sculling about in a boat.

"Kirwan had loaded provisions,
A mast and a sail and some twine;
Three breakers of water, an axe and a gun,
Some rum and a barrel of wine.

"For hours he circled the flotsam,
Calling each man by his name;
Three men he plucked from a watery grave,
Shouting until darkness came.

"The morning found three of them sleeping,
While Kirwan kept true to the course;
Raindrops were falling and swell waves were formed,
As the wind started rising in force.

"By mid day a gale was raging,
The tiny boat tossed like a pea;
Waves came like mountains to swallow them whole,
Two were swept into the sea.

"Now there was just Ned and Kirwan,
Caught in the ocean's distress;
The two of them knew that the chances were slim,
The boat was a splintering mess.

"The boat's tiny mast was uprooted,
She started to ship swirling brine;
Then one vicious wave struck the boat with full force,
Stoving the barrel of wine.

"Kirwan struck out for the barrel,
Ripping the lid from the cask;
He shouted to Ned they must bale for their lives,
Grimly they started the task.

"Somehow their strength didn't falter,
How they managed it God only knew;
The boat soldiered on through the teeth of the storm,
Somehow they brought the boat through.

"For three days and nights they were battered,
Driven by breath of typhoon;
The fourth night saw both of them slumped on the floor,
Under the light of the moon.

"The days were now long hot and thirsty,
The breakers had started to leak;
Slowly they moved with no sail and no oar,
Drifting for many a week.

"Ned grew so feeble and sickly,
Baked by the hot southern sun;
Kirwan prayed hard for deliverance from high,
But deliv'rance came there none.

"In the bows of the boat Kirwan rested,
By the tiller was lying poor Ned;
Kirwan brought over the last drop of water,
To find his companion was dead.

"He lifted his eyes up to heaven,
Cursing as sailormen do;
Despair filled his heart and he thought he must die,
Just like the rest of the crew.

"The boat gave a lurch in the water,
Aground on a large coral reef;
An Island nearby with a beach and some palms,
Kirwan was filled with relief."

My father's rich tones had been fading,
I know now I'd fallen asleep;
The next day my father was lost out at sea,
Claimed by the watery deep.

I never did hear all the ballad,
But such as I know I tell you;
For you are my child and this birthright is yours,
As far as I know it is true.

I look up with tender affection,
My treasure's asleep in the bed;
I wonder how much of the ballad was heard,
Whilst fighting those eyelids of lead!

-ooOOoo-

ALPHA AND OMEGA

You start in the gutter of cities and towns,
With rubbish to choke up your flow,
The winos and urchins go by with their frowns,
Yet few think to find where you go.
Dead cabbage and bottles disfigure your face,
You're dank and unloved in your grime,
Rainbows of oil spin their glistering lace,
Strawberry coils dressed in lime.

Soot-blackened bricks speak of endless travails,
Crowding you in twixt the walls;
Bridges stoop low like satanic brick snails,
Skulking beneath smoky shawls.
Outlets from factories spew out their waste,
Coke cans float idly by,
Even the air has a bitter-sweet taste,
Under the grit-laden sky.

Your journey continues through housing estates,
Children and puppy dogs play;
The old folk sit watching by back garden gates,
Serenely you pass on your way.
Your towpath is clearer and bedded with stones,
Trees can be seen on the bank;
The children skim pebbles while dogs gnaw their bones,
Brambles grow rank upon rank.

Your water grows purer and fish may be seen,
Power lines hum overhead;
Gone are the waste pipes and slick oily sheen,
Here there are mayflies instead.
A mile further on and a boatyard is found,
Barges chug by in the sun;
Fishermen dream of the roach that abound,
As ground bait goes in by the ton.

Out past the houses your journey goes on,
Leaving the bustle and noise,
Slowly it's noticed the people have gone,
Here are the countryside's joys.
The bridges are ramshackle ivied and old,
Set to a backcloth of green;
Their undersides bristle in lichen and mould,
Carpet where brickwork had been.

Dragonflies hunt down their meals on the wing,
Making the most of the day;
Birds hop round hedgerows and cheerfully sing,
Tempting the hiker to stay.
Rabbits sneak down from their burrows to drink,
Then scurry away like a flash;
Flowers give glimpses of yellow and pink,
Waving their blooms like a sash.

The kingfisher's blur paints a streak in the air,
Quickness deceiving the eye;
Bumble bees fuss like old maids at the fair,
Lest one blossom passes them by.
A curious cow pokes her head round a tree,
Watching the boats as they pass;
And having decided there's nothing to see,
She goes back to munching the grass.

Great timbered locks are protesting with strain,
Boats are tied up by the pub;
The fields nearby hold vast oceans of grain,
And there is a fox with her cub;
Another fox seeks out his prey in the wheat,
But the evening rabbit has ran;
It's terribly English and cannot be beat,
Considering where we began.

-oooOooo-

DUCKS AND DRAKES (AND CHILTERN HUNDREDS)

The civil servant hunted through the budgetary accounts,
Highways were expensive – as he knew;
But why was Holte Construction paid such boggling amounts?
Then it came – a bolt straight from the blue.

The minister was shaking at the import of the news,
The civil servants ambled through the mess;
And while the wretched minister was quaking in his shoes,
They calmly leaked a memo to the press.

Sir Robert was the departmental secretary to Holte,
Holte was treading water (in manure);
Sir Robert made sure everyone knew he was not at fault,
Then leaked another memo (to be sure).

Holte was with the cabinet who felt the end was near,
As he spoke he fiddled with his nose;
"If I must resign I'll lose a hundred K a year,
Still, there's always Brussels I suppose?"

Behind the tinted glasses the PM remained aloof,
Soon there was a by-election due;
He knew that in his desk there lurked a wealth of solid proof,
And made a note to leak a memo too.

And so the wretched minister was stabbed from every side,
When he hit the floor they used the boot;
They all knew he wanted to protect his worthless hide,
And so began the Whitehall turkey shoot!

Outside the Fleet Street jackals checked for papers in the bin,
Sir Robert left for Spain to get a tan;
The marbled halls were silent as the ministries dug in,
Waiting for the shit to hit the fan.

The PM called a hasty conf''rence far away in France,
The Chancellor had fled to Timbuktu;
Holte was in the firing line and never stood a chance,
The civil service knew just what to do.

Perkins phoned up Mason who spoke urgently with Jess,
Lowther cleaned the files 'til they were white;
Sir Ian Muir at once arranged a conf'rence for the press,
And leaked another memo – just for spite!

A flock of junior ministers kept calling number ten,
Jess had taken all phones off the hook;
The corridors of power leaked a memo yet again,
Muir consulted with his little book.

The party chairman cursed because the phone began to bleat,
The call-girl dressed in rubber stayed her cane;
But Muir's voice was assuring him that Holte would take the heat,
The chairman put his gasmask on again.

Way down in sleepy Devon the Home Secretary was high,
Muir spoke most distinctly down the line;
"Lock 'em up – degenerates!" was the only slurred reply,
As he caught the opium bottle just in time.

Sir Ian had but one more call, his conscience to appease,
The Attorney General answered in his car;
But he wasn't really listening for his mind was filled with sleaze,
Whilst driving to the local lap dance bar.

So when the conference ended and the press went home to tea,
When the dust had settled for a while;
Holte (who took the *Chiltern Hundreds*) went for M.E.P.,
And made himself another little pile.

Sir Robert flew back home and carried on just as before,
The PM came back too, to number ten;
There's sex and drugs (<u>and</u> rock and roll!) behind that shiny door,
But they make damned sure they won't get caught again!
-oo0Ooo-

INDEPENDENT MEANS

A product of the middle class with independent means,
Armani shirt and *Gucci* shoes with best designer jeans;
He went to university where father paid his place,
Equipped to deal with everything except the human race.
He pulls up in the Gti outside his Docklands flat,
And looks around him just to check he's where he thinks he's at;
His mind is fully occupied with what to have for lunch,
The world is busy working – they're such an oddball bunch!
Even all his friends have jobs so he must eat alone,
And wasting no more time he jumps straight on the mobile phone;
The table's booked at *Anton's* by the time he's at his floor,
He's settled on the Chablis by the time he's at his door;
The shower does the business and refreshed he starts to dress,
Adding just a hint of scent to make the ladies guess.
The Rolex snaps about his wrist as wistfully he smiles,
Planning yet another night spent out upon the tiles;
He wonders at the little people eking out their lives,
Drove on drove of busy bees who swarm about their hives;
What a dull and pointless way to squander all your days,
It's far more fun to view the world through alcoholic haze;
What can match the finest food washed down with Scotch and gin?
And who would dare reproach him for the states that he gets in?
His body's low on alcohol for now his brain won't stop,
Whilst stepping to the pavement he espies a waiting cop;
Perhaps he'll get a taxi as so often he's advised,
It really would be awkward if he should be breathalysed;
He steps right out into the road a speeding cab to hail,
Oh what an awkward moment for the cabby's brakes to fail;
The hospital worked day and night to save his fractured spine,
An overburdened surgeon tried to set it back in line;
It's hard to be a paraplegic barely past your teens,
For now he'll never truly know what *'independent'* means.

-oo0Ooo-

GHOSTS

I took my country's quarrels and I turned them into mine,
Though at the time I didn't think it so;
Yet I agreed to kill and maim by signing on the line,
For I was young back then and didn't know.
Each night I clutch the bottle with the sleeping tablets in,
Yet sleep is not the answer to my prayer;
Dreaming is the price I pay, the wages of my sin,
Ghostly faces haunt me with their stare.

Desperate and reproachful are the glances that they give,
Many are the times they plague my thought;
The question never varies for they ask why I still live,
What can I say – how may I retort?
They come to me in sleepless nights and float inside my head,
Seeing not the bullet as it goes;
Unwitting smiles or abject fear on faces of the dead,
Bodies jerking in the final throes.

My dreams are often shattered by staccato bursts of fire,
Muzzle flashes give that vivid glare;
The shapeless lumps in body bags are lowered in the mire,
As overhead the one-o-five shells tear.
The scant reward was paltry when compared to what I've done,
Each bloodied scene I witnessed in the field;
My stock-in trade was killing and my tool a loaded gun,
When I took aim their fate was surely sealed.

I've seen the bullet strike its mark observing their surprise,
And heard them choke and drown in their own blood;
I've watched the failing flick'ring light go out behind their eyes,
And known them blown to pieces where they stood.
I pray that God forgives me for the beating hearts I've stilled,
Even though twas in my country's name;
For I cannot forget each face of every man I've killed,
Though at the time I thought it was a game.

-ooOOOoo-

EYE OF THE BEHOLDER

It cuts a swathe by night and day
To march upon its stony way,
Across the fields and round the town
It travels in its concrete gown,
A mesmerising snake of grey.

From here it seems to scar the land
Yet from above its woven band
Of silken tarmac forms in lanes,
A spider's web of busy veins,
Each hill is cut and river spanned.

A thing of beauty? Well not quite
But take another look at night,
When concrete bridges hide their shame,
The world lights up in twelve-volt flame
Of flashing amber, red, and white.

The endless miles hum idly by
Beneath the brooding sleeping sky,
Long distance drivers ply their trade
Within the realm of night's deep shade,
Each passing truck a moaning sigh.

The flitting lights go on for miles
Atop the sleeping concrete piles,
Each one a firefly in the dance
To hold the watcher in a trance,
Enthralled by traffic's droning wiles.

If you could speak what tales you'd tell,
Of peaceful nights and days of hell,
You've carried hope and joy and pain
Through heat and frost and slashing rain,
And sped them on, their souls to sell.

Yet all's forgiven in the dark
For now your form is not so stark,
The fiery pinpricks wend their way
Along the sullen motorway,
Each a vital, living spark.

The night makes speed a heady brew,
Yet there is lurking out of view
A predator who stalks the gloom,
Harbinger of licence doom,
With rending fangs of flashing blue.

The errant driver sees too late
His fast approaching sealéd fate,
The kill is sure and quickly made,
Prey brought down and swiftly flayed
By expert servants of the state.

Indifferent, concrete piles observe
Each new day's test of skill and nerve,
The tarmac jungle's pathways close
Upon the cars in shining rows,
Which only get what they deserve.

-ooOOoo-

HAPPY SMILING FACES

How often they garble how lucky I am,
Grinning as slyly they wink;
But really they don't care a tuppeny damn,
Smiling as slowly I sink.
Because I'm now single they say that I'm blessed,
Cautiously sipping their tea;
The look in my eyes says I'm hardly impressed,
They cannot begin to know me.

How lucky it is I'm surrounded by friends,
Keeping me cheerful in style;
How long will it be 'til this bonhomie ends?
Just leave me alone for a while.
This pathway must take me wherever it leads,
And if I want peace let me be;
Solitude sometimes is one of my needs,
Truly they cannot know me.

In an hour or less they'll go home to their wives,
I shall be here on my own;
And while they get on with the rest of their lives,
I'll sit and stare at the phone.
The scenes of my love and my life seem to pass,
Black and white stills that I see;
Moments of love held forever in glass,
If only they'd learn to know me.

God only knows how much damage they've wrought,
Or how much they'll do if they try;
Sometimes I sit all alone deep in thought,
Sometimes I just sit and cry.
They tally her faults then present me the bill,
Saying 'it's best to be free,'
Yet the feelings I had for her live with me still,
Surely they ought to know me?

Their faces are happy and smiling and bright,
Keeping their spectres at bay;
But my spirits haunt me the length of each night,
Depression each mile of the day.
I miss her sweet laughter and tender caress,
Her green eyes as deep as the sea;
She's hurt me more deeply than they'll ever guess,
Maybe they shouldn't know me.

'It's good to see smiles on your face' they intone,
As gaily they head for the door;
I bid them adieu with my grin set in stone,
Concealing emotion so raw.
The door echoes shut as they head for their cars,
I smile as I pocket the key;
For all they're aware I could well be from Mars,
And I realise they'll *never* know me.

-ooOOoo-

THE DEVIL'S VEST

Twas a windy night with a moon full bright and an evil, eerie air;
Behind the hill where the breeze was still a shape was moving there;
Betwixt the stream and the moonlight's gleam the campfire's glow was red;
The old man's eyes seemed to tell him lies, and so he shook his head;
A hooded shape in a flowing cape came stalking down the track;
The man looked on 'til hope was gone and a chill ran up his back;
Through wisps of smoke the Devil spoke, eyes a flaming bright;
"Stand aside old man while you still can – you're not my prey tonight!"

The old man knew with insight true, that Satan meant his son;
With the desperate speed of urgent need he seized his loaded gun;
Without delay he made his way to where the young boy slept;
The wind rose high'r as round the fire, Satan slowly crept;
Now the Devil thought to have some sport, and break the old man's mind;
But the old man's head was filled instead with plans of a different kind;
"I'll say it clear – the boy stays here" was heard the old man's yell;
"Just one more pace towards his space and I'll blow you back to hell!"

Satan scowled then faintly growled but came no closer yet;
Full well he saw the set of jaw and feared his match he'd met;
He sized the man as a wicked plan was hatching in his head;
To leave the child while he beguiled the wizened man instead.
"I'll wager gold that you're too old to fire that weapon straight;"
But Satan's shout was filled with doubt lest that should be his fate;
His crafty eyes surveyed the prize still soundly sleeping near;
But the old man's squint was hard as flint with ne'er a trace of fear.

"I'll not ask twice so name your price, I'll grant you your desire,"
But the gun moved not one single jot as the old man made to fire;
The devil flinched as back he inched to where the shadows lay;
In his black mind he tried to find the right things he should say.
The man tracked round with ne'er a sound and strained his eyes to see;
The gun was cocked and aim was locked to where the fiend should be;
"Now quell your haste and do not waste the offer I have made,"
But the man's resolve did not dissolve in promises of trade.

The man took up his metal cup and filled it from his tin;
Then dashed it down, his face a frown as the water turned to gin;
He stilled a sigh though his thirst was high, and kept his watchful guard;
As the breezes keened his body leaned for the night was long and hard;
The devil's grin was cruel and thin as dancing forms appeared;
Each demon's breath was foul as death as evilly they leered;
When the old man saw full half a score were gathered on the hill,
They shook their spears with mocking jeers, yet the man defied them still.

The clamour grew and Satan knew that most men would not stand;
But no matter what the man moved not and his knife was in his hand;
Demons leapt as others crept expecting him to run,
Yet the old man stood to sell his blood beside his sleeping son;
The knife flashed quick as he made it stick within a scaly breast;
Its blade was keen and blood flowed green as the old man gave his best;
Knife bit deep on hillside steep and demons turned to flee;
The man dealt death with rasping breath and a furious, dreadful glee.

From 'neath his cowl a wailing howl escaped from Satan's lips;
Its withering sound sped o'er the ground with the sting of flailing whips;
Beyond the fire the Devil's ire was brewing like a storm;
The lightning flew in bolts of blue about the Devil's form;
Sheets of rain like stabs of pain came lancing from the sky;
Wind swirled round in gusts of sound then quavered to a sigh;
Then at last the maelstrom passed to stillness of the night;
It left no sign nor whimpering whine of Satan's livid spite.

The devil spoke behind his cloak of darkness in the bush;
His voice was hard and cracked and tarred across the icy hush;
"There's no respite 'til dawn's red light is rising in the east,
There is no peace and no release, in the presence of the beast;
The mark of fear is ever near when I am close at hand,
And to my will I'll break you still – against me none may stand;
So say your prayers for no man cares if you should live or die;
There's none can help your precious whelp, nor grant him life save
I!"

The old man knew the words were true and all the reasons why;
But with delight he saw the sight of daybreak in the sky;
A bird's sweet song trilled clear and long to greet the coming day;
As with a flash the gun's sharp crash sent vengeance on its way.
If you should chance a merry dance with Satan down below;
Don't mind your feet or skip the beat, just tell him that you know;
Ignore the imps – ask for a glimpse of the wound that's on his chest;
If he says no it's then you'll know just why he wears that vest!

-ooOOOoo-

GOODBYE

Cry me an ocean of hot stinging tears,
Weep me a river to mourn past its weirs,
Slay me the good things in life with a glance,
Then pin me the fruit of all hope on a lance;
I dwelt for a time in the sun of your smile,
Knowing that you would be gone in a while;
Straining to stretch every second with you,
Dreading the moment we must bid adieu.

Dry up the lakes and lay low every hill,
Tear up the skies, bid the oceans be still;
Rip out the still-beating heart of *Desire*
And brand it with irons, a thief and a liar;
Melt down the trumpets which signalled our dawn,
Bring sackcloth and ashes and leave me to mourn
In peace, to lift gently the veil of white lace,
Stricken and crushed by your beautiful face.

There's no rhyme or reason for you were so young,
Your page was unturned, your ballad unsung;
So slowly you slipped as your life ebbed away,
The light ever fainter with each passing day;
Trade my life for yours and don't tally the cost,
For my soul is dying, my future is lost;
My tears on your face shine as jewels where they lie,
As stooping, I tenderly kiss you goodbye.

-ooO0Ooo-

CHRISTMAS IN THE COUNTRY

Beneath the lowering damson sky
The halo'd moon goes scurrying by,
And through the piercing nightly freeze
The woodsmoke capers on the breeze,
Before it dances off to die.

The northern airs blow stark and chill
To where the snowflakes dance and thrill,
Each breathless eddy builds a mound
Then flattens it with ne'er a sound,
A virgin cloak o'er dale and hill.

The morn reveals the faerie lands
Wherein Jack Frost with stealthy hands,
Has weaved his spell on fields of white
While captive breath so diamond bright,
Floats through the air in silvered strands.

The mill wheel groans beneath the weight,
The stream is frozen smooth as slate;
Each ditch and hole inlaid with silk,
The rutted lane awash with milk,
The pageantry of nature's state.

In every corner of the shire
From stately hall to humble byre,
Wherever man or beast is found,
The chill comes creeping through the ground,
And men draw closer to the fire.

Down by the pond the horses neigh
While cheerful chattering Robins play,
Swooping from the laden bough
To land upon the snow-clad plough,
And watch the cattle chew their hay.

The bells ring out so brittle-bright
In spires, aflame with frosty light;
The sleepy village has awoke
Each pew bedecked with cheerful folk,
For Jesus Christ is born tonight.

As evening shows her purple hue
And dusk cocoons the churchyard yew,
The parson in his surplice stands,
The congregation join their hands,
To hail man's saviour, born anew,

-oo0O0oo-

GONE

The sun has lost its lustre and the clouds are glowering grey,
The wind is keening through the pines to make the grasses sway;
Black ribbons flutter in the breeze around the fresh-dug ground,
Black boots crunch on the gravel path with melancholy sound.
She was my sun, my moon, my stars, but now the world is dark,
No longer shall we walk the woods and listen to the lark.
Tear down the trees, scorch the grass, slay birds upon the wing,
For nevermore shall beauty bide in any living thing.
The lakes must all be drained away, the rivers all run dry,
I wish no touch of comfort as the desolate days go by;
No longer shall I hear her laugh or feel her loving hand,
For she has gone, and left me in a strange unearthly land.
Each new day's dawn is cancelled through the coming bitter years,
For I must surely founder in this sea of burning tears.
She was my world, my light and warmth, my sky and sea and air,
And now the world is finished with for I no longer care;
Bleach the soil and quench the lights, choke the ocean's swell,
So joy and love and breath can perish 'neath the tolling bell.
Let all the music cease to play, stop all the children singing,
So everyone may hearken to the death knell's solemn ringing;
Make all the laughter go away – slay merriment at birth,
Draw shut the leaden curtains – there's no more use for mirth.
Chase out with lightning bolts of fire on solid blocks of stone,
The message that my love is gone, a cut unto the bone;
Stand back and let the mountains fall, they have no further worth,
As love, clad in her wooden shrine, is lowered in the earth.

-ooOOOoo-

CRY FOR HELP

The sun was weak this morning with the taste of watered tea,
The day was dim and overcast which made it hard to see;
I cannot quite recall what hour I staggered from my bed,
I only hear the whisperings which sigh within my head;
The lilting tones of madness touch upon the nerve that's raw,
Until I shake and shiver and the sweat streams from each pore.
The bitter tang of hemlock has been welling in my throat,
At last I've found my moment as I write my farewell note;
In crowing tones I'm told my moods are fraudulent and base,
Once too often have they forced a smile upon my face.
My heart is black and vacant while my brain in torment boils;
Insanity the artist paints in lurid glowing oils;
The missus ran away with someone new to who knows where,
And social workers took the kids and put them into care;
I took the bottle's solace 'til the cash was drank away,
And now my sodden mind can't take another twisted day;
The final straw was loaded and my mind just had to break,
Blade has fondled wrist to make my blood a crimson lake.
They stole my dreams and sold my soul to keep themselves amused,
Yet in the dock of conscience each and all shall stand accused.
How strange is this sensation and how warmly spreads the stain,
This numbness in my arms and legs permits no hint of pain;
How slowly does my body sink into this creeping cold,
How light are sleep's embracing arms before death takes a hold;
I tried so hard to tell them that I couldn't carry on,
And now their help is not required for soon I will be gone.
Away from all the cutting words and cruelties I despise;
Beyond the clouds which fog my thoughts and twist them into lies.
To circumstance I'm wedded and to fortune I'm a slave,
Far better to be out of reach within my yawning grave.

-ooOOoo-

THE GODDESS AND THE STRING

Come dance like a fool in the footlights of life,
Capering round in a trance;
The puppet knows nothing of who pulls the strings,
Only the steps of the dance.

My passions were stolen and sold on the block,
Or maybe they never were real;
But who pulls the strings from the gantry so dark?
And whose is the touch that I feel?

It's she picks me up when the show's at an end,
To pack me away in my case;
Yet always she hides what my soul yearns to know,
With never a glimpse of her face.

There must be a God (for who else pulls the strings?)
And someone must light up the stage;
But star of the show is the fool on the wires,
A marionette in a cage.

Deep in my mind there's a shadow of thought,
A time when the passion was there;
Perchance there was light in these dead wooden eyes,
And maybe a glimmer of care.

My thoughts are so bruised that I'm wooden and stiff,
My varnish is cracked by the rain;
'Could it yet be' says a voice in my ear,
'That she'll be my goddess again?'

Some say there's nothing unless you have love,
Others that hate is the king;
But when you have neither then life is a sham,
Unless you are pulling the string.

-oo0O0oo-

60 YEARS ON

The sparkling water dances 'cross the shoals of sand below,
And gurgles over pebbles as it smoothes them with its flow;
The willow stands in silence as it weeps upon the grass,
Its dripping branches drink their fill, then let the water pass,
To where the banks meander at the water's chuckling ease,
It's here the forest's gentle gloom is rustling in the breeze;
The shafts of sunlight lancing down in spears of golden light,
Marking where we used to sit, the water bubbling bright.
The mossy banks look golden 'neath that canopy of green,
Each drop of dew a precious jewel of glittering silver sheen;
I would that I could sit there as we oft were wont to do,
The sunbeams playing in your hair, and in your eyes so blue.
These portraits never leave me and I know they never will,
For as I gaze into the stream, your face is with me still;
Oh can it be so long ago, that day you grasped my hand
And pulled me laughing, through the shallows, barefoot in the sand?
Each drop of spray a diamond as it caught the summer sun,
In a stream of sparkling silver, whose course had yet to run.
The summer days were longer then, and hotter so it seems,
And by the stream I hold you still, inviolate in my dreams;
Enchanted were those days we spent beneath the beech and pine,
A treasure-trove of mem'ries as your hand slipped into mine.
Time has turned the pages as life's stream goes babbling on,
Each twisting turn and bubbling shoal is whisp'ring that you're gone;
Yet by the dancing water's noise, together we will be,
Running, laughing, hand in hand, where life's stream meets the sea.

-ooOOoo-

Somewhere in Oxfordshire – near the village of Hornton where my grandfather was born – are two hills, known locally as 'North' and 'Tirpitz' with a gurgling stream at the bottom. As a child in the late 1960's my grandfather would occasionally take me there and show me where he 'courted' my granny, and she would tell me of the mad rides down the hillsides he inflicted on her in a motorcycle combination. Of course there was much more to it than I realised at that tender age, and it wasn't until later life I came to understand just what it was he was showing me. My grandfather was to all outward appearances unremarkable, yet to those who knew him he was truly the most exceptional man – a role model I am afraid I could never emulate. He worshipped my grandmother for more than 60 years of marriage and this work is dedicated to them.

BEYOND PRICE

What is far more valuable than diamonds set in gold?
 What's the most expensive thing that any man can hold?
The one thing that no man may buy, be he a mighty king,
 More precious than the universe, a bright and blazing thing.

Its worth is far beyond a price that mortal man may find,
 It isn't cold and hard like jewels, only warm and kind;
It can't be sold or traded yet its power is complete,
 And once alight it burns with fiery incandescent heat.

This thing is often searched for yet to many it's denied,
 To gain it men have searched in vain and multitudes have died;
It warms the blood and brings fresh life to both the young and old,
 Yet some have tried to stifle it beneath the lies they've told.

Bad men try to murder it and good men wonder why,
 But though it's often threatened it can never truly die;
The foolish try to purchase it but they can never see,
 Unless it's given freely it's as worthless as can be.

More durable than works of art it lasts a whole life long,
 No one understands it – but it's never, ever wrong;
Some say it's a fallacy and some say it's surreal,
 But yours is worth the world to me for that is how I feel.

It's found in summer sunshine and in tulips in the spring,
 It's found in blood-red roses and the heady scents they bring;
It's found in gentle raindrops as they plummet from above,
 But most of all look in my eyes and there you'll find my love.

-oo0Oooo-

MAIDEN OF THE NIGHT

What is this thing that ails your mind each time you try to sleep?
 A gnawing boring nagging doubt that burrows fast and deep;
This thing cannot be side-stepped and it will not be denied,
 And all must one day walk aboard its roller coaster ride.
What is this icy shaft of fear which plunges through men's hearts?
 The fog-bank of oblivion is where the nightmare starts;
It preys each night upon the thoughts colliding in your head,
 Rending with its talons as it stalks about your bed.
This thing is what you fear the most – I fear it too my friend,
 There's no way to avoid it and it's waiting at the end;
It strikes the young and slays the old and carries off the ill,
 Quenching breath and closing eyes, limbs are cold and still.
This thing will never leave you, yet take succour in the day,
 For night time finds a mind obsessed, in paranoid decay;
Yet all may sit and contemplate the dread which none may miss,
 Ushered in on silken wings to plant the poisoned kiss.
What is this thing that ails your mind each time you try to sleep?
 A chilling maid in frozen robes to plunge the dagger deep;
Her touch brings immobility her glance will steal your breath,
 And if you really want to know, the maiden's name is *Death*.

-ooOOoo-

59

JUST BEFORE THE DAWN

Whatever great disasters have befallen you of late,
Remember it's not aimed at you – it's just a quirk of fate;
When next door's dog has bitten gran and grandpa's fallen ill,
The wife has found she's pregnant 'cos she didn't take her pill;
The next door's dog gets out again to excavate your lawn,
Remember – it is always darkest just before the dawn!

Granny's got her fingers stuck beneath the blender's hood,
Little Katie pressed the switch and now there's lots of blood;
Grandpa's vomit blocked the loo so now the water pours,
Your teenage daughter backed the car straight through the garage doors;
The bank has sent a letter to complain you're overdrawn,
Remember that the darkest hour is just before the dawn!

Outside it's in the nineties and the world is going brown,
The central heating's gone berserk – you cannot shut it down;
Little Katie's jammed the switch with chewing gum and sweets,
And now the wretched bloody thing just heats and heats and heats.
There's vomit on the sofa and your temper's getting worn,
Remember that the lowest point is just before the dawn!

By now the bathroom carpet has the texture of a bog,
Grandpa's just been vomiting all over next door's dog;
Aunt Edna's come to visit with her manners so bizarre,
And now the binmen drive the dustcart straight into her car.
There's madness and there's mayhem and you wish you'd not been born,
Remember that the blackest moment's just before the dawn!

The day consists of trouble and around you all is strife,
The hanging basket in the porch has fallen on the wife;
You tried to clean the greenhouse but your foot slipped through a pane,
Who's ripped the washing on the line – it's next door's dog again!
You're wedded to misfortune and to chance you are a pawn,
Remember it is ever grimmest just before the dawn!

Grandpa's lost his bearings and has vomited on you,
And when you go to check the meal there's vomit in the stew;
You take it to the patio to cool it for the bin,
But as you turn and walk away – next door's dog dives in.
Aunt Edna's got a paddy on and glares at you with scorn,
Remember that the clouds are thickest just before the dawn!

Now Granny's got it in her head that she must clear the loo,
And with her bandaged fingers she is scooping out the goo;
Next door's dog has cleared the bowl and gives it one last lick,
Then wanders in the kitchen where the bloody thing is sick.
Little Katie's howling 'cos she's stood upon a thorn,
Remember that the heart is faintest just before the dawn!

The workload now is lighter – little Katie's gone to bed,
And grandpa's stopped the vomiting – he's breaking wind instead;
The smell is foul and putrid but you bear it as you should,
While scrubbing out the blender to remove dear granny's blood.
You're ready for a breakdown and your face is pale and drawn,
Remember that the light is dimmest just before the dawn!

Grandpa's stripped the telly out and done a proper job,
Aunt Edna says *'he's round the bend'* and slowly starts to sob;
Granny takes exception and she thumps her round the head,
Grandpa says he wants to go and fix the garden shed.
Aunt Edna's nose is bleeding and her favourite dress is torn,
Remember it is always gloomy just before the dawn!

Granny's on the sofa and she's saying not a word,
Her hands are smelling funny and the bandages are furred;
Grandpa's snoring deeply but that's not his loudest noise,
And as you leave to make the tea you slip on Katie's toys.
You start to laugh hysterically for hope is now forlorn,
You've only just begun to see – you'll never make the dawn!

-oo0Oooo-

ON MY WAY

The whims of fortune steer our way
No matter what men do or say;
Each gust of wind – each surge of tide,
Will clash and smash and override
The best laid plans of yesterday.

Yet down the path we all must go,
To stumble blindly in the flow,
And none content with what they need,
Most are burdened by their greed,
The few by what they think they know.

So where, o pilgrim on life's road
May one lay down the heavy load?
O where may one find sweet release
To stay and lay and take some ease?
Must always shoulders be so bowed?

Men's sinews strain and muscles tear
Beneath the burdens that they bear;
Through avarice and pride and scorn
The load is always singly borne,
And far too valuable to share.

Awake! Awake! You're all but blind
And being led by your own kind,
This lofty path on which we tread
Has either side deep pits of dread,
With shattered dreams each one is lined.

They sweetly call on either hand
Of Dollar, Pound or Krugerrand,
The bridge is down not far ahead
So why not tarry here instead?
The flames of greed are subtly fanned.

Speak not to me of golden gain,
Of diamond dew and silver rain;
Begone foul fiend from Hades torn,
Of Scylla and Charybdis born,
For each brings nought but hurt and pain.

Of all the crimes proscribed by law
The worst, it seems, is to be poor;
But in his way the pauper's blessed
He has no coinage to invest,
And therefore keeps his spirit pure.

The wealthy man may travel fast
While poor men make the journey last,
And as the rich will feast and dine
On sweetmeats and the reddest wine,
The pauper chews his small repast.

Yet pathways have an end some day,
To cross the Styx we all must pay,
But coins are not the only fare
And as the rich will first be there,
Please tell him that I'm on my way.

-oo0Ooo-

A PRAYER FOR DAYBREAK

If you should chance to pass by me before the dawn's red glow,
Please wake me with your gentle touch, before you turn to go;
And if I should cry out in fear and anguish at the pain,
Then grant me just one moment's peace in all this mud and rain.
Across the wire, behind the guns, is death for all to see,
The other side of no-man's land my maker waits for me.
So wake me with a whispered word, my duty to perform,
And let me feel your presence, throughout the coming storm.
These boys are young and frightened and I hope they all get by,
But come the cold harsh morning light, most of them will die.
Do not forget to wake me when the sun looms bright and large,
That I may blow my whistle, and lead the bloody charge;
The frozen pools in no-man's land sit waiting for the dawn,
To bear their silent witness as man's folly is reborn;
As boots scrape on the firing step and rifles are unslung,
The weary climb the ladders – rung by muddy rung.
The rats watch with indiff'rence as they scurry from the trench,
To see the blood and guts and gore and revel in the stench.
Tonight I'll snatch my fitful sleep amidst the rotten ooze,
I pray to dream of emptiness whilst sipping at my booze;
But come the morning bright and hard the rum will do no good,
Between the scorched and shattered trees, each will spill his blood.
The flower of youth is rendered up to a hail of whining lead,
Each phantom bullet finds its mark as I lie in this bed;
So don't forget to rouse me for it's early I must wake,
Is it too much to ask, dear Lord, for daylight not to break?

-oo0Ooo-

"Lest we forget, 1914-18"

SELLING ONESELF

I earn my living on my back which must make me a whore,
Occasionally, with special tools I charge a little more;
I'll tell you yours is special though at present it is ill,
But if you let me play with it I'll give you such a thrill;
Now yours is not as others are – it varies from the norm,
Just place it in my skilful hands – I'll get it to perform;
The bill could be expensive and I'll need it overnight,
But it's your prize possession so you've got to do this right.
I'll give you back the thrusting power missing for so long,
With special lubrication to ensure it's smooth and strong;
Now if you want a *'quickie'* I'll be finished in a tick,
But let me do the full routine – I promise you it's slick!
So let me touch your working parts and tune them for response,
No one else supplies the driving pleasure that it wants;
I'll test your vital spark and check the body while I'm there,
You may as well surrender it into my loving care;
I'll tease your pumping turbo 'til the pressure's up to par,
'Cos I'm a good mechanic – and it's such a sexy car!

*Mechanics do it from underneath (with special tools!)

-ooOOoo-

65

THIEPVAL (1916)

The pale rays of dawn kiss the bayonet tips,
The big guns speak out spewing death from their lips;
The trenches are lined with the pawns of the game,
The faces have changed but the eyes are the same.
From Fricourt to Ypres, from Albert to Loos,
The pawns have been slaughtered in orderly queues;
The men pray to God as the shells whistle past,
Each knows this morning may well be his last.
The force of the barrage just beggars belief,
And *Death* stalks the line like a crafty old thief;
He follows me still down from Flanders to France,
Where mud pools will choke and the bullets will dance.
The ground writhes and boils in the tempest of spite,
Grotesquely attesting the howitzer's might;
Soon now the call on this raped summer's morn,
And it's over the top where all hope is foresworn.
He follows me onwards awaiting his chance,
As bold ranks of khaki are told to advance;
He's there in the craters, the slope of the hill,
My breath comes in sobs yet he follows me still.
A harsh and cruel mistress this lady called *war*,
If *peace* be a maiden then *war* is a whore;
Tempting with glory and glimpses of might,
Yet baring her dirk for the stab in the night.
Her pillow's barbed wire and her mattress is mud,
What you thought was silk is an ocean of blood;
She takes from your soul with her words so profound,
Whilst stealthily digging your hole in the ground.
Hell's orchestra plays but we're well on our way,
Our wounded fall writhing to die where they lay;
The battered remains of our line are a mess,
Thinned by machine gun's impartial caress.

I know he's still there in the hole to the right,
Taking men's souls like a thief in the night;
Harry's gone down with a lingering groan,
And looking about me I see I'm alone;
O mother please help me, I don't want to die,
I can't feel the pain and I want to know why:
His hand's on my shoulder, I stifle a shout.
But all noise has stopped – the lights have gone out.

-oo0Ooo-

THE BALANCE

In life's rushing street 'twixt the truth and the lies
We each to the top of the heap try to rise,
While amongst all the flotsam and jetsam we fight,
Biting and clawing our way to the sight
Of riches in gold and in silver and jewel,
Never believing ourselves to be cruel
Or heartless or devious, serving our ends,
Waiting to strike, for our lifestyle depends
Like the hunter, on what can be viewed through the sight,
Endlessly prowling like jackals at night.

Yet viewed very simply life's wicked and base,
No time for regrets in the heat of the race,
For each second counts on the mobile phone,
Selling each other with cold hearts of stone,
While wondering blankly at what we've become,
A credit or debit in life's massive sum;
Remember the boy that you bullied at school,
Or the dunce in the corner you thought was a fool,
Like the new boy you harried and teased like the rest,
Simply because he was shabbily dressed.

You think you are better, or cleverer as such,
But you and I really don't change very much,
For our human condition's a sordid affair,
To the victor the spoils, to the vanquished despair.
We slay what we love for we're blind in our greed,
Compassion is dying and we watch it bleed;
And now love lies bleeding all over the earth,
Because of the way we assess a man's worth;
Man's spirit is killed with a soul-rending sound,
And when weighed in the balance, it's wanting we're found.

-oo0Ooo-

BORN OF SUPPLY AND DEMAND

Oft I am found in the taverns and inns,
Courted by fat men with large double chins,
My fee is not high (though my body is nice),
With me you may lie (if you render my price);
With powder and lipstick and perfume I'm armed,
Prepare to be weakened and perfectly charmed;
With pout of red lips and a cute little wave
My waggling hips will ensnare me a slave;
The stockings are sheer and the garter belt tight,
As I stalk for my prey in the heat of the night;
My lips are of crimson, my eyeshadow blue,
Warm in my bed there's a place just for you.
Come take me and love me and service your need,
Crying out loud in your passionate greed;
I'll force you to kneel with a whip in my hand,
Or caress and seduce you – whatever you've planned.
I've lotions and toys and a flat full of fun,
And I'll dress as a maid or a nurse or a nun;
Just pay me my fee and I'll do as you say,
And when you're relieved I will send you away.
I'll give you what you'll never get from your wife,
The things you have dreamed about all of your life;
I'll never be shocked – if you want it just say,
There's all kinds of games that I know how to play.
In leather or rubber and shiny high heels,
No need to be shy – just say how it feels;
I'm just on the job and my conscience is clear,
For men made me this way – didn't you dear?

-ooOOoo-

MEETING A FRIEND

The lushness of the emerald grass, the washed out sapphire sky,
Bowls of food for eating, cool water when you're dry;
The other dogs are friendly with their noses to the green,
And in the wood you'll find the biggest sticks you've ever seen;
They float upon the water through the rapids, to be raced,
While in the banks of furze, there are rabbits to be chased;
The stream is never icy, the stones are polished round,
Fish leap in the currents with that flapping splashing sound;
Sometimes it takes hours to investigate the noise,
Often I'm assisted by the other girls and boys;
Tails wag and bums get wet, noses sniff the air,
If we don't find what it is, well, we don't *really* care!
The sun is always shining and there's never any rain,
The joints move free and easy, I'm young and fit again;
There's rubber balls and bags of bones and toys in giant piles,
And when you cross a fence you have to bounce across the stiles;
A dog's work here is never done, there's always more to know,
Somewhere to investigate, somewhere new to go.
I might just chase a butterfly, or pigeons on the wall,
But now my ears have lifted, for I thought I heard you call;
My tail is beating wildly as I head off at a run,
Heading for my shouted name, fur flowing in the sun;
Did you think that when I left, we'd never meet once more?
Never let me lick your face, or take my offered paw?
I revel in my breathless pace, my eyes are fixed on you,
I knew that you would come for me, I knew, I knew, I knew!

-ooOOooo-

FOR JOLLY JACK TAR

The might of old England as proud as can be,
The ships and the men who went off to sea;
With hearts made of oak, with walls made of wood,
To give us our victories, paid for in blood;
Coming back crippled, no legs or no arms,
With no hope of work in the towns and the farms;
Owed a great debt – yet by many ignored,
Until the next time there is need of the sword.

Still we are proud of the battles they won,
Braving the shot – still crewing the gun;
Who were these heroes, ruling the waves?
Some long forgotten in watery graves;
The cannons lie silent the shot flies no more,
No longer the echoes of bloodshed and war;
No more the madness and chill fear of death,
No longer the cutlass' ending of breath.

Nelson and Collingwood heroes may be,
But made by anonymous men of the sea;
The gunner and bosun the master and mate,
Backbone of frigate, brig and first rate;
The pressed man, the felon escaping the rope,
The debtor without any future or hope;
Characters all in the motley array,
Serving The King through the wind and the spray.

Onward they forge through the bitter-cold swell,
Seeking out battle, enduring their hell;
Fisting cold canvas whilst braving the gale,
Sons of Britannia who never would fail;
The ensign is fluttering high on the mast,
'Tis to glory they steer, true to the last;
The canvas may strain and the stays be belayed,
But the bill of the butcher has yet to be paid…

-oo0Ooo-

CHILDREN WITH MATCHES

Though the Devil may sleep with a heart black as soot,
Beware oh my friends there is mischief afoot,
For his thoughts and his dreams are still potent I fear,
And his twisted designs may become all too clear.

To each man his due be it sorrow or woe,
Oft it is wrote ye shall reap what ye sow;
Each child in the crib, be it girl be it boy,
Will bring to the world either sorrow or joy.
The fortunate child pearls of wisdom is shown –
Each taking root 'til the fruits are full grown;
But the child of neglect only apes what it sees,
And all the good seeds are but chaff in the breeze.
Ward ye the child lest it strays from the track,
We all were but children a little while back.

Though the Devil may sleep, he is restless tonight,
With one eye propped open to see what he might;
At Satan's behest comes corruption by day,
And death slinks by night bringing foetid decay.

The child now is growing and learning its mind,
Be it quiet and thoughtful or brash and unkind;
Both are susceptible still, in their youth,
Yet one is more likely to listen to truth;
Fate deals her cards make of them what you will,
One chooses well but neglect chooses ill;
The seeds of destruction are what he has found,
The bitterest seeds you can plant in the ground;
No fruit bring they forth, only hatred and lies,
And should they be ripened then death is the prize.

The Devil has woken and grabbed at his lance,
He slumbers no longer – he's spotted his chance;
He jigs with delight and breaks into a run,
For his seeds have been found and the game has begun.

The children are men and their courses they steer,
One ruled by wisdom the other by fear;
One wanders free in the sun of life's road,
The other's hemmed in by the warrior's code.
An arsenal is built through his fear and mistrust,
Threatening each day to turn mankind to dust;
Not for defence or a cause that is right,
It's just for the glory – the thrill of a fight.
The cards are still turning, now which will he choose?
He thinks he'll win but mankind may just lose.

The Devil is watching as fate deals the hand,
Shaking with laughter as man makes his stand;
The cards start to turn as the tinder is sparked,
For the deck is the Devil's, and each card is marked.

-ooOOOoo-

BEWITCHED

What is this apparition that bedevils every thought?
And how is it you weave the silken net in which I'm caught?
It only took a single glance and I was lost it's true,
Drowning in the oceans of those stunning eyes of blue.
I find that I am dreaming of your velvet honeyed lips,
I want to put my arms about your slinky swaying hips;
Yet when I'm in a room with you my throat and mouth go dry,
My heart starts pounding madly and I think that I shall die.
I know you like me also for I've seen that little look,
Yet still I wriggle, helpless on your shiny fishing hook;
You must know you have caught me 'cos I know you've seen me glance,
But I do not know how to start this ritual courtship dance.
How hot and bright and glowing is this star to which I'm hitched,
I feel just like a schoolboy who has surely been bewitched;
The magic that you practice is a long-lost mystic art,
Guiding straight along its beam, the point of Cupid's dart.
You are my darling angel from the wispy clouds above,
How fervently I'm praying that you'll take a chance on love;
I want to hold and cosset you and keep you safe and sound,
Yet I am almost frightened of these feelings I have found.
The first time that I saw you, you were wearing lilywhite,
You stole my soul and made me gasp and set my heart alight;
The second time I saw you I was shocked to see you here,
My mind went into meltdown just because you were so near;
And just in case you're not quite sure exactly who you are,
For you're the gorgeous woman with the very sexy car!

-ooOOoo-

DAYDREAMING

A bright summer's morn in the valley,
The odour of poppy and pine,
Walking the woods is young Sally,
The girl that will one day be mine;
Her hair is a chestnut perfection,
The girl has such beauty and grace;
This love is a creeping infection,
Brought on by the sight of her face.
I would that my heart here could tarry,
To sit on the banks of the pool;
A kiss for the girl I will marry,
And maybe a kiss for the fool.
Her gown is a green inspiration,
Ebbing and flowing like wine;
Her face is God's own pure creation,
Silk skin like the grape on the vine.
The soft arms are warmly enfolding,
Her kiss tastes of peaches and cream,
But where is the girl I was holding?
Oh Sally, you're only a dream!

-oo0Ooo-

WHAT AM I?

Alone and aloof I will hunt in the sea,
My cousin he hunts on the land;
The souls of the living to eternity
I take with my impartial hand.

I'm evil and cruel caring not where I strike
A terror, of men's greed I'm spawned;
Created to kill whomsoever I like,
Silent and deadly and horned.

My breath is a fire that scorches the soul,
Destruction that bursts from within;
To slay without mercy or thought is my goal,
Oblivion lurks 'neath my skin.

To see me is fear and to touch me is death,
By many I'm cursed as their fate;
For smashing their limbs and quenching their breath –
Though of course, for them, it's too late.

I reap from the young and I harvest the old,
Twixt friend and foe draw I no line;
I prey on the coward and hunt down the bold –
For I am an enemy mine.

-ooOOoo-

A HYMN FOR EDWIN

A shroud of grey engulfs the mill and washes out the reeds,
While down upon the valley's slope it chuckles as it feeds
Upon the last few remnants of the ruined castle wall,
Bewitching every lichened stone the silver tendrils fall.
Yet dark and looming in the fog a gloomy island stands,
Alone, forbidding, silent, awash in silv'ry bands.
Deep in its heart sleeps Edwin as the mists swirl all around,
Yet they dare not disturb him in his Saxon burial mound;
For though his spirit slumbers and his body is decayed,
The essence of his spirit calls, a force to be obeyed;
For Edwin was a mighty lord whose lands he held in thrall,
Strong yet just and fair of face, broad and standing tall.
One day 'tis said that Edwin will return and fight the foe,
Who came in ships across the sea and laid young Edwin low;
They say the mist will turn to blood and smoke will hang like breath,
The moon shall strike a thousand blades, each dispensing death;
The valley's sides shall echo and the arrows fall like rain,
When Edwin's vengeful spirit comes to claim his hall again.

A shroud of grey engulfs the mill and flows across the stream,
And as it dances by the mound the moonlight makes it gleam,
Like fiery silver dragon's breath, alive yet cold as stone,
And through the chilly air is heard a quiet mournful moan.
The little hollow by the bridge is filled with silvery light,
With baleful eyes an owl is watching, guardian of the night.
The sturdy oaks and elms have felt the trembling of the ground,
The very earth is singing low, the hymn of Edwin's mound;
The hedgerows add their lighter tone to make the hymn complete,
As through the ground it travels with a vibrance clear and sweet.
The wandering stream sings out the words, a minstrel she will be,
'Oh Edwin, Edwin, sleep no more, your people wait for thee!'
In mother earth's cathedral is the glorious swell of song,
A psalm of praise and summoning for one who slumbered long.
A shroud of grey is cast aside cascading down the slope,
The trees and hedgerows hold their breath, a pause of silent hope;
Atop the mound the figure stands, surveying all the land,
The moonlight sparkling on the sword grasped firmly in his hand.

-ooO0Ooo-

MAN'S BEST FRIEND

I've never asked for anything except for love and care,
And in return I'll give you all I've got;
I know that I'm not perfect with my messy matted hair,
Yet I am quite contented with my lot.
I never asked for anything – not even to be born,
So why is it I'm hungry and I'm sick?
I'm never any trouble and my love to you is sworn,
So why is it you beat me with that stick?
You know I'll never leave you – even though you cause me pain,
Although I whine, it's only 'cos I'm bruised;
And even as you kick me for your pleasure once again,
I love you – even though I am abused.
You may have made me fear you but my hate you'll never earn,
I'd never hurt you – why do you hurt me?
And if you would but feed me I'd be fit and quick to learn,
Service with aplomb and loyalty.
I'd love and guard and worship you right into my old age,
And even give my life to save you pain;
What must I do to please you and prevent your drunken rage?
And will I spend my life here in the rain?

-ooOOoo-

NIGHT WATCHMAN

The night is clear, the frost is hard, above the stars are bright,
The rigging sighs and creaks and groans, but yet the wind is light.
Alone, above the swaying deck – a hundred feet or more,
A sailor crouches on the yard, frozen to the core.
He wonders how much longer, before the dawn will break;
Before his shipmates climb aloft, their turn at watch to take.

The ship is small, the mast so high, he cannot see a thing,
The icy blackness closes in, the wind she starts to sing.
Her melody is almost sweet, a lullaby for sleep,
A thousand miles or more to go, across the ocean deep.
The sea's caress is gentle, despite the bitter cold;
The ship's a real lady now – no matter that she's old.

The swaying mast, the freezing spray, all lost in sleep's embrace,
In Jimmy's violent vivid dreams, there comes a friendly face.
A comrade from a bloody past, now resting 'neath the sea,
A visage warm and friendly now, the way it used to be.
The lonely watchmen searches, his vigil to enforce;
Below him is a man o' war, upon her plotted course.

Stays are taught, the pendant's straight, sails protesting loud,
The bowsprit plunges down each trough, emerging wet but proud.
The old girl's seen a hundred fights and come through every one,
Remembering the thunder and the faces now long gone.
The lonely watchman glances back, upon his face a smile,
As dawn's pink face is in the east, her rays in single file.

The sleeping sailor, stirring now, his clothes all stiff and damp,
Eyes are bleary red and sore, limbs are wracked with cramp;
Yet nonetheless the ship is safe, the watch was ably kept,
The lonely watchman's eyes were sure, as Jimmy deeply slept.
The masthead now is empty – apart from Jimmy Swift,
An old friend kept his watch last night, a final parting gift.

-oo0Ooo-

CHILD OF MISFORTUNE

Whatever you do and wherever you go,
Remember my child – I told you so!

The place of your birth is no longer the same
Regarded by others with pity and shame;
So work hard at school then get out if you can,
For this is no life for a civilised man;
The factories have died for the boom is no more,
The people are sullen and shabby and poor;
Because you're my child I speak only the truth,
The men here are savage, the women uncouth.

Whoever you meet and whatever you see,
I pray it is better for you than for me.

The crime on the streets is a sight to behold,
It's shameful to need and a sin to be old;
The language now spoken is violence and pain,
And slowly it spreads like a stark vivid stain;
This city is rotting and reeks of decay,
With harlots by night and the pushers by day;
Once men worked lathes to make things you could use,
But now they sell pensions and burgers and booze.

Wherever you go and however you fare,
No matter how far I will always be there.

My child I have told you the truths I have found,
The facts are all straight and the reasoning sound,
You're all that I have and to me you are dear,
It grieves me to say that you mustn't stay here;
The wide world is beckoning loud in its song,
And holding you here would be selfish and wrong;
Forgive me my weakness for wishing you near,
When the cities explode I want you to be clear.

Whoever you meet and whatever you do,
You know I will always be thinking of you.

Work fairly for pay but enjoy what you earn,
Never forget how to use what you learn,
False wisdom is common and cheaply it's bought,
While pearls of true wisdom aren't easily caught;
One day when you're older you'll see I was right,
In building this bridge from the dark to the light,
Get out of this slum for this town's a disgrace,
The meek may inherit – but not in this place.

God keep you and guard you by day and by night,
And help you to choose only that which is right.

-ooOOoo-

SOMEWHERE IN A FOREST

The raindrops plummet down,
Each one bedecked in crystal gown,
Alive with vital glistening light,
Ten million raindrops gleaming bright,
This world of men will surely drown.

The sodden earth is drenched,
The grass and trees once parched now quenched,
Deep down the roots lie tranquil still,
Untouched by man's pervading ill,
About their neighbours tightly clenched.

The stream is nature's wine
For ancient oak and gangling pine,
Yet where the water lays her jewels
Are gangs of men with iron tools,
Cantank'rous mules drawn up in line.

O what is this we see?
How can this desecration be?
Where once were hues of green and brown,
The oak and pine come crashing down,
Despite the firmest guarantee.

Heed not the men of lies,
Truth whispers low when she replies,
Not always is she understood,
Oft hacked down in pools of blood,
By assassins in their drab disguise.

-ooO0Ooo-

ONE WE LOST

O brave and noble guardian,
O symbol of the free,
How came you to be stricken
In the sight of victory?

You were the nation's sweetheart,
With mighty heart of steel;
With every inch kept spick and span
From fighting top to keel.

Your claws were sharp and mighty,
Their reach was sure and long;
And though you were no longer young
Your heart was true and strong.

You fought upon the slate-grey sea,
You fought with grace and pride;
Where none may yield and cry for quarter,
None may run and hide.

The sea breeze whispers gently,
On *Holland's* flag she'll play;
As *'Hood'* steams on into the dawn
This fateful morn in May.

-ooOOoo-

THE SHIP

Morn's veins in crimson silk are bound,
The seashore awakes and the morning is found,
Westerly breezes sing out their lament,
Waves lap the beach their life forces spent,
Whisp'ring with barely a sound.

Pebbles roll churlishly round in the rip,
The driftwood is caught in the sand's golden grip,
The headland drinks deep in the salt laden-spume,
Flooding the air with its mineral perfume,
And cloaked in the mist lies the ship.

Her timbers are barnacled rotten and old,
Her cordage is mildewed, her sails green with mould,
Her rudder is seized with the passage of time,
Her masts crack'd and twisted her bell green with lime,
Her crew to the devil was sold.

A long line of captains have bartered her soul,
Exploiting her worth 'til the coming of coal,
Most faithful of lovers, she stayed 'til the end,
Until she's alone with no crew to attend,
Closing her days on the shoal.

Her ratlines have rotted to gossamer thread,
The bosun is drunk and the lookout's abed;
No caulking is left twixt the seams of the deck,
And down on the chart she is marked as a wreck,
A cable nor' east of the head.

Yet strangely the wreckers have stayed well away,
And no one comes near – even during the day,
By night time strange noises are heard from her hold,
And spine chilling stories of demons are told,
By locals who live round the bay.

They say that her captains are held there in chains,
Along with her crews and their ill-gotten gains,
Their spirits are wracked with the need to be free,
Yet something still holds them in foul penury,
Within her decaying remains.

-oo0Ooo-

THE UNEMPLOYED PHILOSOPHER

Throughout the days I wander as a captive in my jail,
Clinging to a beam of light and dreading should it fail;
About me the philosophers debate the world's affairs,
With bated breath I listen to assorted fears and cares.
The ozone layer's far too thin, my benefit is late,
And armageddon's coming – all we have to do is wait;
The price of *weed* is going up, I don't know how I cope,
Might even have to get a job – still there's always hope.

Philosophers are always there to set the world to rights,
Cerebrally imbalanced views attaining dizzy heights;
The state should give them extra cash to fund profound research,
The intellectually challenged view of law and state and church.
Ideas come forth in torrents for their minds are now in spate,
Each more flawed than that before, a fearsome character trait;
The world could be a better place bereft of fault or flaw,
If only they could get more cash to buy some extra *'draw'*.

The air we breathe is stale and foul, I think I'll move away,
And one day I may do some work – maybe – just not today;
Oh – can I bum a cigarette? Oh thanks I'll pay you back,
But maybe not for several months – I feel a little slack.
Hard work and strife is not for him – he has too much to do,
And if you feed him cups of tea he'll stick to you like glue;
The world's a cruel unfeeling place and life is just a cheat,
Beware the *Dole Philosopher* – there's one right up your street!

-ooOOoo-

THE TRAVELLER

Many fields have I crossed, with ditches and dykes before me,
Splashing my muddy way through gorse and bramble to be here.
Many times have I been hungry and cold, sodden with fatigue.
Food is scarce, kind words scarcer still from our masters
Yet still we march, fiends in human form, mindless yet fell
Devouring all who would stand in our way.
With clenched teeth I have heaved my load across this foreign land
Eyeing the great men on their chargers as they splash past.
I sleep in the fields, the stars my blanket, the earth my bed;
There are one hundred sticks upon my back, each with its barb
Polished, sharpened, guided by goose quills, powered by hatred.
Tomorrow I shall draw my bow.
Many shall be by foemen, many shall seek to end my wretched life,
All who see me shall despise me for a coarse, common fellow;
A peasant who tills the land in time of peace, and dies no better
Than a cur, aged and toothless and witless in my years.
Yet me and mine shall fall upon the enemy with dreadful fury
Reaping the harvest of death.
I shall strain the sinews of malice as with the draw of the string
Is sent the messenger of oblivion, straight to my enemy's heart.

-oo0Ooo-

WINSTON

Exalted by the masses and acclaimed both far and wide,
In strident tones you'd lecture and chastise;
You shone forth as a beacon from your pedestal of pride,
Greatness ringing from your words so wise.
You focused all our hopes and fears to forge a mighty sword,
A symbol of defiance in the night;
With guile you trapped the moonbeams in a net of silken cord,
You took our souls and purged them in the light.
Wherever men would gather you were greatest of the great,
Bewitching all about you with your art;
And with your words you left us hanging breathless on our fate,
Dreading lest the silken cord should part.
All my life you've been the grail I've worshipped from afar,
I knew that you could never fall from grace,
And just as we believed you would you raised a shining star,
A lighthouse to the English speaking race.
For though all Europe groaned beneath the madman's crushing
heel,
You never shirked as captain of the boat;
His ranting threats were answered by the gleam of Sheffield steel,
And by the waves that serve us as our moat.
Throughout the dazzling pages of our island's history long,
A finer chapter never shall be told;
The man who fought with nothing to defeat such dreadful wrong,
To hold aloft the shining sword of old.

-oo0O0oo-

TRACK RECORD

Surrounded by the worker ants, a humming in my head,
It's only seven thirty and I should be still in bed;
But now the bell is screeching and I must be at my place,
For another day's survival in the human bloody race.
Without a thought I fit the nuts, it's automatic – see?
My brain will never function much before I've drunk my tea;
Yet if the foreman spies my mug concealed behind the rack –
It's in the office for a caution – *'no drinks on the track'*.
Around me bedlam comes alive with hammer blows and squeals;
Wearily I heft the air wrench fitting on the wheels.
I wonder if the Pharoah's slaves were treated much like this?
I bet they never had to get permission for a piss;
But pyramids are not like cars produced at frantic rates,
Dropping off production lines in wooden export crates.
Motoring for the masses – one a minute if we're quick,
I hate the sight of motor cars they make me bleedin' sick!
A glance along the metal snake and what is it I see?
A hundred shining steel cars waiting just for me
To fit the gleaming alloy wheels and tighten all day long;
Accompanied by rushing air – the impact wrench's song.
The in-laws will be down this week, her dad's a real pest,
Talking all so lah-de-dah, I wish he'd take a rest;
The bugger's started showing off about his brand-new car,
I did the wheels on that one mate – I wouldn't trust it far!

-ooOOOoo-

TO WHOM IT MAY CONCERN

Why am I here on this speeding carousel?
Have you no soothing words, no tale to tell?
When I begged you answer you simply smiled,
You always make me hesitant, as a child;
I languish in the shadows enduring your scorn,
Each screaming tensioned nerve so finely drawn;
For each sarcastic jibe fresh from your lips,
I have no sharp retort – no cutting quips;
To you I am ignorant, dishevelled and unkempt,
For in your eyes there is only harsh contempt;
Why have you barred the portal – let me drift,
When opening the gate is in your gift?
Whatever wrong I've wrought can not have earned
The brightly blazing bridges you have burned.
Supreme in your assurance you decree,
I have no part in your society;
This inky blackness has no focal point,
No rusted locks, no crumbling mortar joint
In which to thrust the crowbar of despair,
No dangling rope no rotted wooden stair.
Condemned am I watching from without,
Consumed by fear and riddled with self doubt;
Revile me as you will for year on year,
Next time you spare a thought, I'll still be here;
In truth, there's nowhere else for me to go,
But that is something you already know.

-ooOOoo-

BEHIND THE CURTAIN

It's just a fine lace curtain that obscures the watcher's view
And keeps the timeless mystery of the place we're heading to:
The threads of silken gossamer cling softly to the air,
To form their gentle barrier across the winding stair.
The gentle kiss of finely woven threads hold back the sight,
While imagination's inner sense can just make out a light;
Just because you cannot see me 'twixt the tendrils' screen,
Don't think for a second that your leaden steps aren't seen.
From my side of the curtain I see every step you take,
I hold your hand 'til sleep arrives and kiss you as you wake;
I see each daily trial and the burdens you must bear,
When sorrows call and tears fall you know that I am there.
When your next step's uncertain and the future seems bereft,
I'll guide you through the noisome dark for I have never left;
I'm with you as you stumble through the field to walk the dog,
And sitting right beside you as you're driving in the fog;
I'll smile when you are laughing and I'll hold you when you're ill,
You know I will be watching out, **for I am with you still.**

-oo0Ooo-

ABOUT THE AUTHOR

Barry Peabody lives on a croft near a small coastal village on the Moray Firth in Scotland with the dogs and the wife, where he tries - often successfully - to hide from the world. He has a passion for 20th Century military history, especially WWI and WWII, and writes poetry in order to impress people. So far this has achieved only limited success.

GENEVIEVE is his debut novel, available in paperback and Kindle/e-book download at Amazon, Smashwords, Barnes and Noble and all good retailers (and possibly some bad ones too). He is currently writing more: one set in the Spanish civil war (a sequel to Genevieve) and another set in WWII Germany, involving murder, espionage, and the Enigma code machine. There is yet another about the life of a WW2 bomb disposal officer which may eventually see the light of day. He combines a love of fast motorcycles and equally fast boats with scuba diving, and trying desperately to escape from his keyboard.

B R Peabody has a facebook page, but refuses to give his first name in case they finally track him down and make him work for a living again...

Available in paperback from Amazon worldwide - simply search "B R Peabody"

Also available in E-Book formats to download for Kindle and E-readers, PC, tablet and smart phone from Amazon, Kobo, I-Books, Barnes & Noble and Smashwords.

Printed in Poland
by Amazon Fulfillment
Poland Sp. z o.o., Wrocław